LAUGHING MATTERS

HOLIDAY JOKES

Compiled by Pam Rosenberg   Illustrated by Patrick Girouard

Special thanks to Katie Cottrell for her assistance in compiling source materials.

Published in the United States of America by The Child's World®
P.O. Box 326, Chanhassen, MN 55317-0326
800-599-READ
www.childsworld.com

Acknowledgments
The Child's World®: Mary Berendes, Publishing Director

Editorial Directions, Inc.: E. Russell Primm, Editorial Director and
Line Editor; Katie Marsico, Assistant Editor; Matthew Messbarger,
Editorial Assistant; Susan Hindman and Susan Ashley, Proofreaders

The Design Lab: Kathleen Petelinsek, Designer and Page Production

Library of Congress Cataloging-in-Publication Data
Rosenberg, Pam.
  Holiday jokes / compiled by Pam Rosenberg ; illustrated by
Patrick Girouard.
      p. cm. — (Laughing matters)
   Summary: Simple jokes and riddles about common holidays.
   ISBN 1-59296-074-X (alk. paper)
   1. Holidays—Juvenile humor. 2. Wit and humor, Juvenile. 3. Riddles,
Juvenile. [1. Holidays—Humor. 2. Jokes. 3. Riddles.] I. Girouard, Patrick, ill.
II. Title. III. Series.
PN6231.H547 R68 2004
818'.602—dc22   2003018083

VALENTINE'S DAY

What did one oar say to the other? Can I interest you in a little row-mance?

What did the caveman give his wife on Valentine's Day? Ughs and kisses.

What do you get if you cross Cupid with a baseball player? A glover boy.

Knock knock.
Who's there?
Olive.
Olive who?
Olive you!

What does a carpet salesman give his wife for Valentine's Day? Rugs and kisses.

What do you call a very small valentine? A valentiny.

3

Did you hear about the romance in the tropical fish tank?

 It was a case of guppy love.

How does a valentine act when it's stuck in the freezer?

 Coldhearted.

What did one calculator say to the other calculator?

 How do I love thee? Let me count the ways!

What did the boy octopus say to the girl octopus on Valentine's Day?

 I want to hold your hand, hand, hand, hand, hand, hand, hand, hand.

Did you hear about the guy who promised his girlfriend a diamond for Valentine's Day?

 He took her to the baseball park.

What did the paper clip say to the magnet?

 I find you very attractive.

SAINT PATRICK'S DAY

What does Ireland have more of than any other country? Irishmen.

What would you get if you crossed a leprechaun with a Texan? A pot of chili at the end of the rainbow.

What do you get when two leprechauns have a conversation? A lot of small talk.

What do you get if you cross a leprechaun with a purple dinosaur? Blarney.

What's little and green and stuck to your bumper? A leprechaun who didn't look both ways!

What did one Irish ghost say to the other? Top o' the moaning!

Where would you find a leprechaun baseball team? In the little league.

5

EASTER

Why was the Easter Bunny so upset?
He was having a bad hare day.

What is the Easter Bunny's favorite state capital?
Albunny, New York.

What is the Easter Bunny's favorite sport?
Basketball.

Did you hear about the lady whose house was infested with Easter eggs?
She had to call an eggs-terminator.

What's pink, has five toes, and is carried by the Easter Bunny?
A lucky people's foot.

What do you get if you cross a skunk with a kind of Easter candy?
Smelly beans!

Why did the Easter Bunny go on strike?
He wanted a higher celery.

Knock knock.
Who's there?
Candy.
Candy who?
Candy Easter Bunny carry all those treats in one basket?

Knock knock.
Who's there?
Philip.
Philip who?
Philip my basket with candy.

7

Why is Easter like whipped cream and a cherry?
   Because it's always on a sundae.

Why does Peter Cottontail hop down the bunny trail?
   Because Mr. and Mrs. Cottontail won't let him borrow the car.

What has big ears, brings Easter treats, and goes "hippity-BOOM, hippity-BOOM, hippity-BOOM"?
   The Easter Elephant.

Why did the Easter Bunny have to fire the duck?
   He kept quacking all the eggs.

A man wanted an Easter pet for his daughter. He looked at a baby chick and a baby duck. They were both cute, but he decided to buy the baby chick. Do you know why?
   The baby chick was a little cheeper!

Did you hear about the farmer who fed crayons to his chickens?
He wanted them to lay colored eggs.

FOURTH OF JULY (INDEPENDENCE DAY)

What would you get if you crossed the first signer of the Declaration of Independence with a rooster? John Hancock-a-doodle-doo.

What protest by a group of dogs occurred in 1773? The Boston Flea Party.

What did one flag say to the other flag? Nothing. It just waved.

Which colonists told the most jokes? Punsylvanians.

What was General Washington's favorite tree? The infantry.

What kind of tea did the American colonists thirst for? Liberty.

9

Why is the Liberty Bell like a dropped Easter egg?
 They're both cracked.

How is a healthy person like the United States?
 They both have good constitutions.

What did King George think of the American colonists?
 He thought they were revolting!

What dance was very popular in 1776?
 Indepen-dance.

What ghost haunted King George?
 The spirit of '76.

How was the food at the Fourth of July picnic?
 The hot dogs were bad, but the brats were the wurst!

Why did the duck say "Bang!"
 He was a firequacker.

Why were the early colonists like ants?
 Because they lived in colonies.

Teacher: How did the Founding Fathers decide on our country's flag? Student: They took a flag poll!

What would you get if you crossed one of the Founding Fathers with a famous monster? Benjamin Franklinstein.

HALLOWEEN

Knock knock.
  Who's there?
Ghost.
  Ghost who?
Ghost to show you don't remember my name!

Knock knock.
  Who's there?
Coffin.
  Coffin who?
Coffin from all the dust in here!

Knock knock.
  Who's there?
Freighter.
  Freighter who?
Freighter ghosts, are you?

Knock knock.
  Who's there?
Howie.
  Howie who?
Howie know you're not a ghost?

What did the black cat do when its tail was cut off?
  It went to the re-tail store.

What game do monster children play?
  Hyde and Shriek.

What's 9 feet tall and flies a kite in a rainstorm?
  Benjamin Franklinstein.

What evil crone turns off all the lamps on Halloween?
  The light's witch.

Why did the monsters hang out at the computer store on Halloween?
  So they could bob for Apples.

What do you call a dog owned by Dracula?
  A blood hound.

Why did the vampire baby stop eating baby food?
  He wanted something he could get his teeth into.

Why did the vampire go to the blood bank?
   He wanted to make a withdrawal.

What do you get if you cross Dracula with Sir Lancelot?
   A bite in shining armor.

What's a vampire's favorite sport?
   Bat-minton.

Where does the bride of Frankenstein get
her hair done?
   At the ugly parlor.

What's a vampire's favorite cartoon character?
   Batman.

What did Dr. Frankenstein get when he
put a goldfish brain in the body of a dog?
   I don't know, but it's great at chasing submarines!

What did the witch serve at her Halloween party?
   Spooketti, halloweenies, devil's food cake, and
   booberry pie.

What do you call a person who lives next door to a vampire?
A tasty midnight snack.

Why can't vampires play baseball in the daytime?
Because bats only come out at night.

What do you do with a green monster?
Put it in the sun until it ripens.

15

THANKSGIVING

What do turkeys have that no other birds have?
Baby turkeys.

What's black and white and red all over?
A Pilgrim with a rash.

What do you get if you cross a turkey with an octopus?
Drumsticks for everyone!

What do you get if you cross a turkey with an evil spirit?
A poultrygeist.

What kind of music did Pilgrim bands play?
Plymouth Rock and Roll.

Who's never hungry on Thanksgiving?
The turkey. He's always stuffed.

Why shouldn't you look at the turkey dressing?
It makes her blush.

16

How did Albert Einstein celebrate Thanksgiving?
  He was very thinkful.

What's brown and white and flies all over?
  Thanksgiving turkey when you carve it with a chainsaw!

Why should you never talk like a turkey?
  Because it's bad to use fowl language.

Why was the dog chasing the band in the Thanksgiving parade?
  He wanted to bury the trombones.

Why were the Pilgrims' pants always falling down?
  Because they wore their belt buckles on their hats!

What did the turkey say to the turkey hunter?
  Quack, quack, quack.

What's the best way to stuff a turkey?
  Take him out for pizza and ice cream.

CHRISTMAS

Knock Knock.
Who's there?
Mary.
Mary who?
Mary Christmas!

Knock knock.
Who's there?
Murray.
Murray who?
Murray Christmas to all, and to all a good night!

Knock knock.
Who's there?
Yule.
Yule who?
Yule see Santa soon!

Knock knock.
Who's there?
Dexter.
Dexter who?
Dexter halls with boughs of holly.

19

What did the bald man say when he got a comb for Christmas?
Thanks, I'll never part with it.

What do reindeer say before telling you a joke?
This one will sleigh you!

Where do you find reindeer?
Wherever you left them.

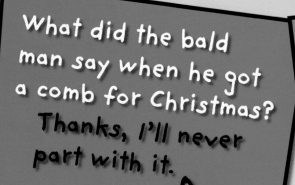

Why was Santa's little helper depressed?
Because he had low elf-esteem.

Why does Santa like to garden?
Because he likes to hoe, hoe, hoe.

What do you get when you cross an apple with a Christmas tree?
A pineapple.

20

How is a flag like Santa Claus?
    They both hang out at the pole.

What happened to the monster
who ate the Christmas tree?
    It had to have a tinselectomy.

What's the difference between
a knight in shining armor and Santa's reindeer?
    One is slaying a dragon, and the others are
    draggin' a sleigh.

What did the monster say when it saw Santa Claus?
    Yum yum.

What do you give a mummy for Christmas?
    Gift wrap.

What goes "Ho, ho, ho swish. Ho, ho, ho, swish"?
    Santa Claus caught in a revolving door.

Why don't you ever hear about Santa's brother?
    He became a ho ho hobo.

BIRTHDAY JOKES

Where do you find a birthday present for a cat?
In a catalog.

What do they serve at birthday parties in heaven?
Angel food cake.

Knock knock.
Who's there?
Mark.
Mark who?
Mark your calendars, my birthday is just around the corner!

What has wings, a long tail, and wears a bow?
A birthday pheasant.

Knock knock.
Who's there?
Wanda.
Wanda who?
Wanda wish you a happy birthday!

How does Moby Dick celebrate his birthday?
He has a whale of a party!

What do you always get on your birthday?
Another year older.

22

A FATHER'S DAY JOKE

Why is it hard to celebrate Father's Day in Egypt? Because there are more mummies than daddies.

A MOTHER'S DAY JOKE

What kind of flowers are perfect for Mother's Day? Chrysanthe-moms.

23

About Patrick Girouard:

Patrick Girouard has been illustrating books for almost 15 years but still looks remarkably lifelike. He loves reading, movies, coffee, robots, a beautiful red-haired lady named Rita, and especially his sons, Marc and Max. Here's an interesting fact: A dog named Sam lives under his drawing board. You can visit him (Patrick, not Sam) at www.pgirouard.com.

About Pam Rosenberg:

Pam Rosenberg is a former junior high school teacher and corporate trainer. She currently works as an author, editor, and the mother of Sarah and Jake. She took on this project as a service to all her fellow parents of young children. At least now their kids will have lots of jokes to choose from when looking for the one they will tell their parents over and over and over again!